MW00934682

the

VISION BOARD CLIP ART BOOK

HEALTH
SELF CARE
+LOVE

volume 1

400+
ELEMENTS

FUTURISTA
INK

★★★★★

Please leave us a review!

Join the Futurista VIP program!
Scan the code and receive **A FREE Vision Board Planner**
when you sign up to be a Futurista VIP. You'll be the first
to know about new listings and shop announcements
and you'll recieve 20% off all purchases in our Etsy Shop.

FREE! 12 steps to put you on the path to powerful manifestation!

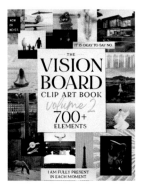

DON'T FORGET TO CHECK OUT *Volume 2*

Modern, minimal and sophisticated. Quiet Luxury at it's best.
Full of gorgeous photos & affirmations.

THE VISION BOARD CLIP ART BOOK HEALTH SELF CARE + LOVE: VOLUME 1
Copyright © 2024 by Futurista Ink. All rights reserved.
No part of this book may be reproduced or transmitted in any form
or by any means without written permission from the publisher.
Images used under license by Shutterstock.com, Freepik.com and Adobe Stock.

New year NEW you

you GOT this

2025

NEW YEAR

this is your year

YES you can

I AM GRATEFUL
FOR MY BODY

I RESPECT MY BODY

I FEEL GOOD
IN MY BODY

I AM GETTING
BETTER EVERY DAY

I HAVE
ABUNDANT ENERGY

I AM HAPPY
& HEALTHY

I LIVE A HEALTHY
LIFESTYLE

I NOURISH MY BODY

I SLEEP WELL

MY BODY IS
HEALTHY & STRONG

I AM HEALED

MY BODY IS ALWAYS
WORKING FOR ME

I AM STRONG

I CAN TAKE
DEEP BREATHS

I CHOOSE PEACE

I ENJOY EATING
NUTRITIOUS FOODS

MY BODY IS A
POWERFUL HEALER

MY BODY IS MY ALLY

BALANCED MEALS
CAN BE SIMPLE

I AM BALANCED

I BELIEVE IN MYSELF.

MOTIVATION

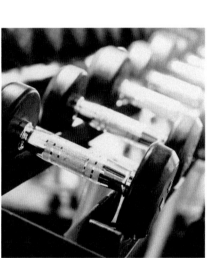

Positive Mind
Good Vibes
Great Life

GOOD
VIBES

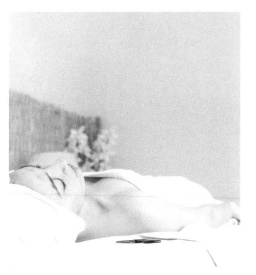

Don't
STOP
UNTIL
you're
PROUD

WORK
OUT

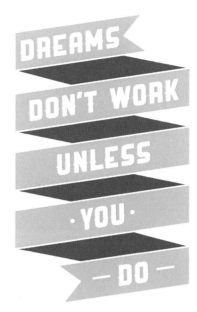
DREAMS DON'T WORK UNLESS ·YOU· — DO —

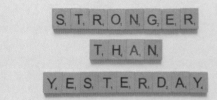
STRONGER THAN YESTERDAY

MAKE TODAY count

Live in the Moment

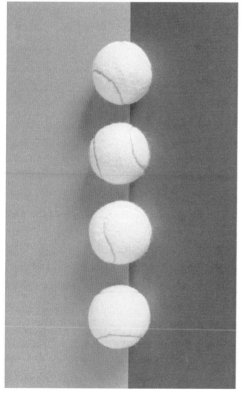

BODY positive

YES you can

GREAT THINGS

NEVER

CAME FROM CONFORT

zones

SORE TODAY
STRONG
tomorrow

EMERGE
ENGAGE
EVOLVE

It's All Good

Be Positive

DON'T STOP
WHEN IT HURTS
—STOP—
WHEN YOU ARE
DONE

drink more water

YOUR BODY your rules

STAY strong

Dear Body, I love you

BREAK THE
RULES

Enjoy every moment

IT'S A VERY
LONG ROAD
BUT IT WILL BE
WORTH IT

I AM LETTING LOVE
INTO MY LIFE.

I AM OPEN & READY
TO FIND TRUE LOVE.

I DESERVE FULFILLING
RELATIONSHIPS.

I AM ENOUGH

MY HEART IS OPEN.

I DESERVE TO RELAX.

REAL LOVE
STARTS WITH ME.

I RELEASE MY PAST
& AM READY
TO FIND LOVE.

I AM WORTHY OF
THE COMPLIMENTS
I RECEIVE.

I CHOOSE JOY
& HAPPINESS.

I AM WORTHY OF
LOVE & CARE.

I AM MORE
THAN MY BODY

IT IS OKAY TO SAY NO.

I DESERVE THE LOVE
I RECEIVE.

LOVE IS MY PRIORITY.

I TAKE BREAKS
WHEN I NEED TO.

I SPREAD LOVE &
IT RETURNS TO ME.

I DESERVE REAL &
AUTHENTIC LOVE.

I AM OPEN TO LOVE
IN ALL FORMS.

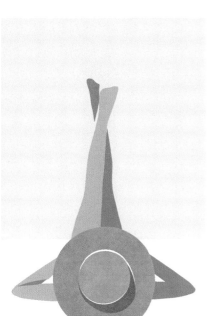

Make Yourself A Priority

Self Love

You ARE THE ARTIST of your own LIFE

SUPER MOM

BODY POSITIVE

Love

YOU
CAN
do it

You Are my
Sunshine

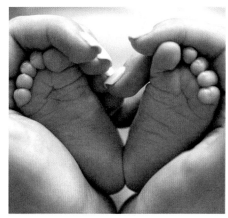

LIVE
IN
WONDER

Live Laugh Love

BIOGRAPHY
adventure
FANTASY
detective stories
Science fictionasy
ROMANCE OF LOVE
Classic
GRAPHIC NOVEL

Love Yourself

be kind
to yourself

Treat Yourself

BE GOOD
BE HAPPY
BE YOURSELF

EMBRACE SELF TRUST

LIVE your STORY

beauty from Ashes

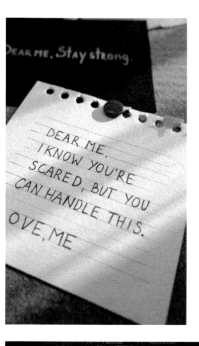

DEAR ME. Stay strong.

—DEAR ME,
I KNOW YOU'RE
SCARED, BUT YOU
CAN HANDLE THIS.

OVE, ME

no bad vibes

celebrete everday

All you need is love

LOVE

BE YOU

SHe WHO is BRAVE is FREE

AMORE · YOU & ME · ONE I LOVE · IT'S LOVE · LOVE YOU · TRUE LOVE

my love

all you need is love

L O V E

LOVE YOU!

Sending all my love

feel the love

let's fall in love

Free love

Share the love

REAL LOVE · SURE LOVE · DEAR ONE · ONLY YOU · SURE LOVE · MY BABY

BRING your Soul

Home sweet home

Positivity is key

DREAM MORE

SEE THE GOOD IN ALL things

TO DO:
1. WAKE UP
2. BE AWESOME

GET IT GIRL

SAY YES

DON'T WORRY BE happy

START TODAY

NeVeR GIVE UP

PERFECTLY Imperfect

Get it Girl

Yes you can

NO BAD VIBES

i am not sure how, but i will

YOU'LL MAKE IT

Be kind to Yourself

ENJOY EVERY DAY

never be afraid of change

IT'S OK TO TAKE A BREAK

PWR

Good see the

WOO HOO

LOVE your SELF

choose LOVE

YOU ARE MADE
of stardust & wishes
AND MAGICAL
things

Love
Your
self

THE WORLD IS FULL
OF WONDERS

OH HAPPY
HAPPY
DAY

don't look
BACK

LOVE
yourself

BEAUTIFUL LADYS
love yourself

WOW

Keep
it
Happy

LITTLE
BOSS

I REALLY
really really really
LOVE YOU

BLOOM
BABY
BLOOM

OH
LA
LA

OH
LA
LA

SING &
DANCE

CHOOSE
LOVE

I STILL LIVE
— WITH MY —
PARENTS

CHE
ERS!

BLAH

Girl Boss

OK, BUT FIRST
a cup of Tea

SING & DANCE

School is cool
YAY

BE HAPPY

YOUNG FREE

LOOKING so PRETTY

KEEP SMILING

COME ON
get Happy

NO DRAMA PLEASE

LOOKING
PRETTY SHARP

all i see is
Magic

COME ON
get
Happy

an apple a day
keeps the doctor away

YAY

Love is in the air

sweet 90s

TOTALY
Adorable

little
PARTY !!!

You are
STRONGER
than you
THINK

COOLEST KID

ever

more

Love

YAY

LIFE IS SHORT
MAKE IT SWEET

Sometimes
ALL YOU NEED
is a
SMILE

make the
PLANET
GREAT
again

BE
KIND

you are made
of sweets

COOL KIDS
NEVER SLEEP

Made in the USA
Las Vegas, NV
29 November 2024

12853262R10036